Country of Warm Snow

Also by Mervyn Taylor

An Island of His Own (1992)
The Goat (1999)
Gone Away (2006)

(published by Junction Press, New York)

No Back Door (2010)
The Waving Gallery (2014)
Voices Carry (2017)

(published by Shearsman Books)

Mervyn Taylor

Country of Warm Snow

Shearsman Books

First published in the United Kingdom in 2020 by
Shearsman Books
PO Box 4239
Swindon
SN3 9FN

Shearsman Books Ltd Registered Office
30–31 St. James Place, Mangotsfield, Bristol BS16 9JB
(this address not for correspondence)

www.shearsman.com

ISBN 978-1-84861-727-8

ACKNOWLEDGMENTS
Grateful acknowledgment is made to the following where these
poems have previously appeared: 'End Days', 'The Wind Dies
Down', and 'Minding the Muse', *2 Bridges Review*; 'Dónde está',
Black Renaissance Noire; 'After the Flood' and 'The Fight', *Boston
Review*; 'Status', 'My Father's Jacket', and 'The Piano Teacher's
Birthday', *Upstreet*; 'Resistance', *Killens Review of Arts & Letters*.

The title is taken from a note by the artist Josep Baqué describing
a piece of his work, which reads, "Interior of some marvelous
large islands at 2 million meters above sea level, unexplored,
uninhabitable by civilized beings, a country of warm snow…".

I wish to thank my friend and fellow poet Susana Case, for her
help and company on the long journey of this book, and my
father, for the place he left me on this island I'll always call home.

Contents

Status	9
City of Tailors	10
Begging a Lodging	11
In Any Country	13
Slow Boy with Harmonica	14
Only Tourists Wear Shirts with Coconut Trees	15
Aretha	16
During Carnival, a Body Washes Ashore at Erin	17
American Girls	18
The Bishops Girl	19
Stone Age	20
Street Clothes	22
Tramcar Sundays	23
The Almond Tree and the Goats	24
The School Gate	25
Swat Valley	26
The Last Villager	27
The Blast	29
Reading with Rukeyser	30
Line by Line	31
Fatherhood	32
Treasury Days	33
Deo's Problems	34
March of the Children	35
The Borough	37
Nation Talk	38
Spirit Animal	39
Crude	41
The Fowl Thief	42
The Barber of East Port of Spain	43
Parables	44
Erosion	45

Once, Carenage	46
Summertime, Brooklyn	47
How It Looked	48
The Fight	49
Woman in the Ringside Seat	50
The Viewing	51
Country of Warm Snow	52
That One	53
Taking My Brother Home	55
She Hasn't Seen Her Son in Years	56
After the Flood	57
End Days	58
The Wind Dies Down	59
Minding the Muse	60
What Now	61
Men Only	62
The Artist as Immigrant	63
Elegy for Saheed Vassell	64
Seven Beauties, Remembered	65
The Side of the Road	67
Beloved	68
The Blind Man Who Saw Through Us	69
Blue Corn	70
Soufrière	72
The Susquehanna	73
The Piano Teacher's Birthday	74
Trouble in Arima	75
Resistance	76
My Father's Jacket	78
Dónde está	79

For my father

Status

Sheriff, the African tailor on Flatbush,
wants to learn English. He can speak
it, but not write it. He's from Conakry,

a word so wonderful I say it again—
Conakry. I offer him slips on which
to write the names of his customers

so he does not mix up the clothes.
When we converse, I find myself
imitating his accent, asking him

where he learned tailoring skills so
remarkable. The space where he sews
is like a cupboard, his four countrymen

squeezed in behind him. We discuss
our cultures, and talk about these
new immigration laws, how they

affect so many. I have no idea what
his status is. I only know that when
I stand before the mirror, my old suit

looks new, and that I would hide him
in my house, and feed him whatever
kind of soup it is they love over there.

City of Tailors

*Belmont, city of tailors seamlessly stitching June
and July together...* —Derek Walcott

The tailor shops have all but disappeared.
Mr. Wilson keeps his half-door open,
and a yard of lining, just in case.

Mackie can't see to thread the needle.
His last suit sits sleeveless on its mannequin,
the customer wearing an old one to the funeral.

Jinx rocks in the gallery of the old folks' home,
regaling them with tales about how
he used to make everyone wait,

while he catnapped over his Singer.
Everyone misses them, especially at Carnival,
when they made the sailor pants wide, and

on Tuesdays, when, dressed to compete,
they went shopping for chalk and fabric,
their seams always unbroken, even now,

as they prepare for that final fitting,
the kerchief in the breast pocket three-
pointed and gray, to match the worsted.

Begging a Lodging

1.
Between two buildings hangs a half-moon,
sparks flying from the fire where we fine-tune
our drums. But no matter how softly we play,

the neighbors call the police. When they come,
we let the light-skinned guy speak for us.
His accent always surprises the Americans.

One homeowner calls us foreign, says we pee on
her flowers. The half-moon lodged between
two walls floats like an island, in and out of focus.

2.
Down in the basements, illegal renters hide.
Tonight, the sky seems smaller, cut into rooms that
share a kitchen, a bathroom at the end of the hall.

When someone asks what happened to so-and-so,
we shake our head, only a week later to hear
he was found dead, half off the bed,

a smell like oysters shucked and gone bad,
in a manila envelope an expired passport and
a heart x-ray, the one he came here with.

3.
One morning I met my cousin on the cheese line
outside a neighborhood Pentecostal church.
When I scolded that it was meant for the poor,

he said, "This country has plenty to go around."
This is why we came, I thought, for the chance to
beg a lodging, for the moon, for the green cheese.

In Any Country
after Roland Guy

There are men like Mahal,
who drive without cars, women
who sew without machines, and
others who lament the one that
take the money and gone Venezuela.

Sometimes they recover, the only
trace of the romance with the
crazy lady being the pain, from
when she turned the penis like a
crank, yelling, *All you men think of*

is sex, sex, sex! Still, you might
one day catch sight of Bobbin,
riding his decorated bike and
crowing like a cock, declaring
his love for a prostitute. Or

poor Spit-in-the-Sea, trudging
down to the beach every morning,
towel over his shoulder as if going
for a swim. But it is only to spit, once,
determined to live up to his name.

Slow Boy with Harmonica

Every morning, in Carnival season, he goes down
to the Promenade where calypsonians entertain,
and Rachel the comedienne tells vulgar jokes.

He remembers a room nearby, where his father
used to visit a lady friend, leaving him with a soda
and sandwich, in a chair just outside her door.

He hopes one day Rachel will ask him what
he thought of the show. And he'll answer,
the harmonica warm in his pocket, that most of all

he enjoyed the anthem, which he was still learning
to play, and that he'd liked her a lot better
before she lost all that weight.

Only Tourists Wear Shirts
with Coconut Trees

They sidle through curio shops behind dark glasses.
They come from Milwaukee, Idaho, Ohio.
They want to know where the zoo is.
They don't understand the phrase,
You getting through?
They've been warned not to go further than
the cathedral, at the far end of the Promenade
from where their cruise ship docked.
On Charlotte Street, some follow a sign
pointing up a narrow flight of stairs.
They come down hours later, having lost
their shirts, the ones with the coconut trees,
the girls with the ukeleles dancing underneath.

Aretha

In Port of Spain the taxi driver said
the woman on the radio singing
"Respect", was Carla Thomas.
She performed here years ago.

That's Aretha, I said.

He said, I meant to say, Aretha,
their voices sound so similar.
She used to sing with Otis.
No, I said, Otis sang with Carla.

Her daddy was Rufus.
He sang "Walking the Dog".
In DC, I saw her play his record
on a jukebox, quarter after quarter.

That Aretha, said the cabbie,
she's something else.

During Carnival,
a Body Washes Ashore at Erin

The streets are full of half-naked bodies,
while this one pops, bloated and dead,
onto the beach, near where he dove.

Who send him, people will say, this time of
year, when current is wild, waves cresting.
Masqueraders jump high, remind us

of a song from long ago: *On Carnival Day,
the beach have to come to town.* They
gyrate in thongs banned from another

island, as images abound on social media,
of behinds being licked, nipples in
someone's mouth, rooms already reserved

for next year. It's hard to identify the local
who tried to escape it, his cheeks puffed
like that minister's who appears to be

smiling all the time. He must have been
a really good swimmer to chance the
lonely fold of water along this stretch

of sand, far from the trumpet's deafening
blast—a small danger by comparison to
the sea, its mouth wide with drownings.

American Girls

They had come up to New York for a wedding, my brother's sister-in-law Salome driving her brand new Cadillac. After the reception, her friend leaned over and asked if I had any gum. "Only what's in my mouth," I said, and she leaned closer, taking it between her teeth.

I thought then, of a letter my friend had written home, about American women, how if they liked you, they'd sleep with you the very first night.

All the way down to DC, where I'd start school in the fall, I observed the new country, the direct way they talked. Like when Lena, in answer to some remark Salome made, said, "I'll take him home when I'm ready. You watch the road."

The Bishops Girl

In her starched uniform,
the blue gore skirt, the jaunty hat,
the tie, she was the pride of the community—
her scholarship, her Senior Cambridge first grade.

But when she got pregnant, the numbers man
frowned. Bubalups pulled her cap down
over her eyes, and Tailor Mackie sighed, as if it
were his daughter, on his most disappointing day.

And after she learned to navigate the clubs,
the rooms of pimps and gamblers,
to put down her books amid whispers
about how smart she once was,

how *promising*, they named her *Zipmouth*,
who hardly spoke as she dismissed them,
three at a time.

Stone Age
for Fatisha

Let's go see if
the turtle's still there
feet planted in concrete squares
its back divided by deep grooves
so however we sat or leaned
we never slid off

What name did we give
the little Puerto Rican kid who
every time he came down the slide
would run back and tell the others
we were kissing

We would forget the hour
to go back to work, the elevator
facing the supervisor's door.
We kept reciting and imagining
that the turtle

together with the other animals
had formed a ring
in the center of the playground
you and I and the children making rhymes
about what it said to the hippo

Let's go see if
they remain as stone as possible
or if when we finally went
back to work they sang what we sang
imitating the way we pursed our lips pretending
not to be on lunch break on W. 17th Street

but a pair on a journey from this planet's beginning
having lost our shells around here somewhere

Street Clothes

In the dream I'm in pajamas on a street
near Brooklyn Hospital, in Fort Greene,
where I once ended up after a panic
attack, a nurse taking the oxygen tube
that wasn't even attached to the tank.

I'm going through my pockets, to see if I
have enough cab fare to get home. On
DeKalb, there are only expensive yellows,
the drivers in those stevedore caps, just
noses showing. They prefer Manhattan.

No one notices me. My pajamas are blue,
with brown stripes; I wonder if they
could be mistaken for casual clothes,
summer wear. At night I would look like
one of those people rescued from fires,

whom firemen throw blankets over, with
apologies for their losses. But by daylight
I'd be taken for some patient who left his
bed, the pressure apparatus pinging,
continuing to register high numbers.

I awake before the guy sweeping out
the deli shoos me away, before I can ask
to use the phone to call someone who'd
come for me, even in dreams. Like you,
who will tell me what it means, asking,
the pajamas, were they dirty or clean?

Tramcar Sundays

We'd sit up front where we could
watch the conductor punch tickets,
a pile of confetti growing at his feet.

I'd keep the stubs and read off
the stops we passed—Chancery,
Victoria, the ink staining my fingers.

We'd listened to the old Queen's Royal
clock chime, lighting up the hours as we
drove by Stollmeyer's Castle. And after

we came to the last stop, the wheels
meshing and grinding, the long, springy
antennae sparking on the cables,

my father would buy us two Cokes at the
Queen's Park Café, and we'd sip slowly,
as he wiped the purple from my hands.

The Almond Tree and the Goats

They stripped the trunk until the tree
looked like an umbrella, my father
under its remaining shade, conductor

turned minder of livestock, a pair of
pens against the fence, pellets of dung
everywhere. He'd rent out the male,

stern men discussing the terms as they
led it by the horns to a female that
would kick the gate to her stall before

growing wall-eyed and still. There was
good money in this. I saw the helpers
sometimes come close to blows, in a

tug-of-war over the branches, De Coteau
picking the tiny leaves, saying they
were the ones the animals loved most.

Meanwhile, my Dad on a low bench
emptied worms from a kid's belly, his
fingers going deep, searching for more.

The School Gate

Before he reached her, her killer had
passed many people: the fishmonger,
whose blade was longer than his;

the Muslim entering the mosque,
turrets gleaming in the sunlight;
a mother hurrying her kids off

to school; the owners of an antique
furniture shop, where he'd
found a rocker to match his chairs.

At the school gate, he passed
the children lined up—boy, girl,
boy, she greeted them, unaware of

his presence until she saw the fear
in their eyes. Then, as they
stood, mouths open, superhero

lunchboxes dangling from their
arms, the children witnessed his
stabbing motion, while she

never screamed, only pointed
at the gate they should go in,
please, dear God, go in. Go in.

Swat Valley

Before the new soldiers, the sergeant
uses a rabbit to demonstrate how to kill
with one's bare hands. He grabs it by

the scruff, and with one quick movement
snaps the neck, whereupon the recruits
jerk, rifle stocks striking the concrete.

Urine runs down the leg of the one at the
far end, as the instructor takes the fur in
his teeth, ripping it from the animal's body,

blood spattering his tunic like a red sash.
In the silence that ensues, there's a gasp,
but none is certain from whom it came.

And the air is leaden, like the soldiers' legs,
so they can't step forward when ordered,
to grasp those downward pointing ears.

The Last Villager

No one knows what's inside
old Isidore's grip. He's not sure
either, being blind and forgetful.

He thinks there's a picture of
Rosanne La Rosa, the day
she helped him put the cross

up on the church, the light
fading fast, so he had to climb
down the ladder in the dark.

When the malaria epidemic
came, it took half the people
in the village, Rosa with them,

filling the cemetery near the
spring that flowed cold and
clear, while plantain overgrew

the hillsides, and soursop
rotted in the gardens. Isidore
and his mother were last

to leave Manantao, that by
now has all but disappeared,
the way back a hidden path,

the sign pointing to nothing
but bush. They say that
parakeets in the trees still

mimic the priests' sonorous
sermons, the woodpeckers
the hammering on the cross.

In the suitcase are the tools
with which he fashioned the
crucifix out of balata wood,

when Rosa tried hard not to
laugh, but did, every time
he missed, hitting his finger.

The Blast

It opened a huge hole on that avenue
known for African boys selling fake
bags, and scarves that, joined, would be

long enough to wrap this city, where
pressure proved too much for an
old pipe and it burst, a young cyclist

pedaling to outrun the asbestos, her
face powdered white. It had been the
kind of summer day that made riders

exit the subway a stop early and stroll,
pausing in front of the building with
grinning gargoyles, wondering who

made them, when the ground shook
and the Africans covered up their goods
and ran, on the lookout for police, or

immigration men. And firetrucks unreeled
their hoses, as tenants fiddled with keys
and tried to calm their dogs, and a crowd

slowly gathered outside Macy's to watch
the hysterical woman going round and
round inside one of the revolving doors.

Reading with Rukeyser

I was looking over my poems
when she said, *May I?*

"Young again and black again"—
Such a lyric line, she offered.

I had heard of her exploits, how
she'd once read outside prison walls
down under, until the gates opened

and the poet-prisoner came out,
proud to meet the lady with the
hawk nose and kind, grey eyes.

I felt her feathers brush
my shoulder, her bird spirit
for a second flying low beside me.

Line by Line

When Brodsky kept us afternoons
poring over poems by Akhmatova,
I admit I understood only half of
what he and the poet were saying,

the island birthright in my bones
withdrawing from the arctic cold of
their verses. And when, frustrated
with our answers, he reiterated his

usual directive—*line by line,* a way of
making us *feel* the frozen arm of the
gulag, only Joel, who was from Maine,
and who'd go back there to die

in his favorite lumberjack shirt, and
Lucie, her ash-blond hair covering
her shoulders till that was all you
saw of her, only those two grew

ecstatic over the word *tundra.* All
I could do when Joseph asked if I
was getting any of this, was stare
at the book, light fading in the fall

evening, and say, yes, exile is difficult,
however we phrase it. It makes one
unbend like a diver at the last minute,
afraid of entering the unfamiliar sea.

Fatherhood
for Ihsan

It helps, if your father's a poet and
read you sonnets, if one happened
to stay in your head, guiding you
through the maze that is life.

If he dedicated one of his books
to you, even if you were too young
to take in a single line, you could
come later to understand the whole
thing was a long apology for what
seemed like selfishness on his part,

the way you yourself are accused
of being distant, always rehearsing
under your breath how a word fits,
compared to another. And though

there are no excuses for letting
my son wait by himself in a motel
for his mother to come from work,
making a new start in California,
no poem worthy of the images

of dunes in the distance, of that
empty pool round back, they
form as if I looked out with you,
the way a poem will lay down lines
for a train to run, and a platform
where we wait, in case one is coming.

Treasury Days
for Peter

Perhaps it's for the best you're not
around today to hear the mistakes
I might make, my memory never as
good as yours when we had to

go over columns of figures, in that
granite building at the bottom
of St. Vincent Street, new clerks in
an old government. That was when

balancing the books was our biggest
problem. That, and liking a woman
whose husband had horses. What was
her name, again? After all these years,

there's no detail you can't recall.
Like the last time we sat—you, me,
and the nurse, around the table
where your meds were lined up

so there'd be no error, so you could
retrieve the one for sugar, the one for
pain—and blind, still picture the shirt
someone on a given day was wearing.

Deo's Problems

At the bank this morning, Deo breaks
the line, telling everyone his troubles.
He shows us property papers, a picture
of the house he'd bought, sight unseen,
from a Miami man. The teller calls,

Next, while Deo, preoccupied, wonders
if he should ask his brothers' advice,
remembering how they cheated him out of
his inheritance, causing him to migrate.
There's a woman who lives near here
who likes him. *Maybe she and I should
marry?* He shows us the blue
plane ticket sticking out of his pocket.

He should go, even if it's just
to see the place. Even the guard
at the entrance, as Deo is leaving, calls
after him, *It's hot. It will remind you of home.*

March of the Children

There are many gods: god of sunlight,
god of the brook, god of night, god of rain;
god of the child who comes to see what I
am doing, god of the mother who cries,

Leave him alone! God in the sulfur of the
match, god in the ashes, god of silence
who lets only the crickets chirp, god who
places antlers on the deer, god of ivory,

and of wood. Good gods, they all crowd
outside our window when we pray, gods
of debate and argument and rhyme, the
gods of fire less inclined to talk, lest they

cause conflagration. They come in answer
to our children's prayers, since it's not the
usual call for sneakers, or a toy or for
a boy to like me, or for longer, thicker hair,

but for an end to war, for god of mongoose
to stop it from killing a snake, for Anansi
to stop telling stories, the schoolyard today
empty as if everyone has a fever, the god

of islands pushing them all together like
desks, so the children can copy from
each other the lesson *On Disobedience*,
on when our children are no longer ours,

so they are free to leave home in a dinghy
and paddle till all the boats are met in the
Ocean of Plastics and from there proceed
to the giant Oil Spill and the ice that melts

like ice cream while we keep saying no
it was the other god we meant, the one
who fixes what we break the one who has
no designation but to see about us fools,

god of enigma god of folly god of cars that
drive themselves god of ducks and deer
crossing the highway have mercy on them
on the children as they feed us in our dotage

wipe our mouths our behinds our slates
clear of wrongdoings, shame and misdeeds,
our money-god the last to come, the one who
called for children to be put in cages, that ungod.

The Borough

Where Sears is now, is where Tilden
Hall used to be, partygoers' shoes
red from the floor polish Hector used.

Grand Tabernacle is where Cat's Hat
stood, floor sinking under the weight
of a hundred dancers. The old Kabuki,

on Ocean Ave., is where the Bad Girls
used to wine*. Ozone Layer is where
the prettiest one suffered an aneurysm.

On any tour of Brooklyn, these places
should be mentioned. They are part
of legend told in a drug dealer's den,

while cranes on Flatbush swing their
heavy loads, and skyscrapers rise and
draw their own conclusions in the air.

* *gyrate.*

Nation Talk

Yuh does thank God yuh bubbies still big…
—Kamau Brathwaite

You mentioned *bubbies*, but no woman
could say you insulted them, or made them
shame, unless they were already ashamed,
of themselves, of their mother and father.

No one could say you made them feel
abandoned, that you saw them crying
and passed them straight, or didn't take
bread from your mouth and give them.

When you sang *Limbo*, we knew full well
it was both dance and prayer you meant,
the face passing an inch below the fiery
bar, legs trembling as we came back up.

And when you saw those heads bob like
coconuts in the Caribbean Sea, separated
from bodies, we knew not to run, but to
wait, till the tide brought them back to us.

Spirit Animal

The spot where I am now,
is where my dad died. I
imagine it's his breath I smell,
his scent, as if he were a wolf,
and I've tracked him here.

I race over my mother's steps,
her fingers rummaging through
places he might have left us
a treasure, such a secret he
kept while building this house,
such a manly thing to do.

I sniff the branches where
his coat might have snagged,
tall firs up against which he
might have rubbed. Instinct
has led me back to the night
he breathed his last, to
the image of him panting,

because I want his struggle
to have been a fierce fight, the
hair on my own body to bristle,
my howl so terrible it will be
heard in the next village, where
they cannot sleep, wondering
what my return means.

I bury my head where his
lapels would have been, I call

his name, Juju, for his wolf
to answer his son's, tonight,
as the world hears, and trembles.

Crude

What type of pitch do we use
that our sidewalks crumble so,
and when we fix them, why do
they sit so high above the road

that the elderly must be helped
down, one trembling leg after
the other? Ah, these dips and
rises, said one tourist, dizzy from

the sun, resting in Cipriani's short
shadow, shirt dark with sweat.
Still, he seems happy, munching
on his doubles, the wife nearby

taking pictures. Tomorrow they'll
visit La Brea. Their guide will explain
the nature of crude, how it glazes
the streets of London, Washington.

But here, it makes turtlebacks
of our lanes, breaks up our step,
as joy does for Miss Dickinson,
my poetry teacher explained.

The Fowl Thief

Barefoot, dressed always in khaki,
when the boys laughed at his skinny
frame, he'd respond, *pukka-pukka*,
the sound cow feet made cooking.

To the lady peering at him under
her house, his fingers around her
Rhode Island's neck, he seemed
better suited to a noble occupation,

like when his long arms whipped
mattress needles through the copra,
causing the fiber to fly, a fine dust
coating his face. Or on Carnival Day,

the only time he wore shoes, sandals
laced to the knee, bronze-tipped spear
held sternly, when he became a
palace guard, in Abyssinia's Royal Court.

The Barber of East Port of Spain

Under some rickety stairs
Hassam cuts hair, he and his
customers ducking when
they hear gunfire.

Upper Nelson is at war
with Lower. It's so stupid,
they agree. Sometimes
he closes his door,

waits for the bullets
to stop. But before
the end of the day,
someone will knock—

Wedding, man. And
Hassam goes to work,
never once nicking anybody.
Never once giving up.

Parables

When my friend LeRoy decided to leave America,
I remember him getting a haircut that last day,
sitting in a chair in the middle of his living room,
the rest of the furniture shipped or sold, only his
plants still hanging in the windows, and from shelves.

I watched the barber take his time, as the sextons
in the churchyard across the street folded their tents,
their parables enticing no more visitors; they carried
poles and canvas carefully, like patients, closing
the heavy church doors behind them. This, I

thought, is the season that marks the end of things.
I remember looking at the bare walls, and LeRoy,
when asked about the plants, saying, *Let them die.*
His paintings, unframed and rolled, were out in
the hallway, packed in long boxes that lay like boats.

Erosion

I'm glad to discover the mountains
of my youth still in place, though
now and then there's a mudslide,
blocking the Lady Young. Yesterday,

a house dropped whole into the sea
at Cedros. I think I may have to return
soon, before more of the island
disappears. I mean the people, too,

like the boy gunned down last week,
traces of whose blood I stepped over
on my way to the terminus, where the
Carenage bus takes forever to come.

Once, Carenage

I liked how easy it was to get there
on the bus from City Gate, how on
the way back, you'd remember details,

like the tree in bloom across from the
police post, the girl in the orange bikini.
The cute ones, you remarked, always

hang with the bad boys. And now you
say you don't recall seabirds walking
on the same spot we had lunch, where

the guy with his brains spilling out in
the picture in the papers has ruined
the boardwalk for everyone, blood

between the planks, the sea coming
in, out there the island of wrecks you
always swim to. Three shot dead, they

say, and one kid, whose breaststroke
we'd admired, now breathing through
a tube, like a scuba diver going under.

Summertime, Brooklyn

In Prospect Park the bridesmaids
pick up their hems and have the photographer
snap them feeding the geese, while the
groomsmen fiddle with their cummerbunds.

In Coney Island, to commemorate the arrival
of Africans to these shores, their descendants
fling flowers into the surf, the Ferris wheel
in the background turning slowly.

On Flatbush Ave., barbers have their hands full
shaving heads for the summer. New mothers poke
their heads and their strollers through the door,
looking for the men they love,

or else they go shopping for candles to replace
the ones dying out in the shrines of Bed-Stuy,
as out of Prospect comes another limo, the third
this week, the bride waving, the geese getting fat.

How It Looked
for Ansil & Margaret

All the years you were away
I kept that photo you sent,
standing by a big black car
with your wife Margaret,

you in a long winter coat, she
in black fur. It was a small, grey
snapshot, with a white border,
snow all around, on the tires,

on the windscreen, on your
shiny black shoes, and on
the windowsills of buildings
behind you. I thought the car

was yours. Years later, when
you came home, you said
it wasn't. It just happened to be
on this wide street in Brooklyn

where the picture was taken,
where the snow seemed like it
would never melt, and a good-
looking guy and a pretty lady

stopped and posed, both their
coats fell past their knees,
and all the world for a second
looked like it belonged to them.

The Fight
for Keith and Ansil

The ad at Barclays Center is for
a fight between Deontay Wilder
and Luis Ortiz, and I thought you
guys would have liked to catch this,

arguing who had the uppercut,
who had the better swing,
that against Ali, neither would've
stood a chance. These are the

delights of the fight game:
the lacing up of the gloves,
the referee, the ringside crowd.
The sign has me thinking now

about how Ansil must have gone
headfirst down those basement
steps, his grandson yelling, "Get up,
Grandpa, get up!" The way we call

for the champ to get up, while the
corner man, who knows better,
says, "Stay down, son, stay down,"
a bet none of us would have won.

Woman in the Ringside Seat

She came to all of Ali's fights,
hoping one night to see him
finally get knocked out.
She tasted his sweat
flying everywhere, heard
his interview with
the showman announcer,
the Anti-American
oath he swore, his
declaration of objection,
his name-change. Honestly,
she'd preferred Cassius,
the artful dodge of Clay,
the malleable nature of it,
the speed of his boots,
as he used the rope.
But the conviction in those
gloves, in the Muslim name,
victory after victory, made
her gasp, pay to see him
defeated. And those awful
heroic couplets he
composed! She cursed
the night he added her
to one of his verses, butterfly,
bee, the demise of all species,
the pretty, and the not-so.

The Viewing

In the middle of the eulogy,
a gas bubble erupts near
my heart, the nerve

in my elbow sending its
funny message to my brain.
Up on the screen, there's

Scrapper, the deceased,
under a thick moustache
grinning broadly, as was

always his way, even when
he needed two canes, and
couldn't stand for long.

"What a privilege to carry
everything to God in prayer,"
I find myself singing, so

loudly, a lady in the front
turns around, the feather
on her black hat trembling.

Country of Warm Snow
for Courtenay

You stopped by, feet swollen
from sleeping sitting up. When
I think of how we entered this city,

separating through the streets
in the months after, I picture the
state you had gotten lost in, east,

west, perhaps one of the dry
ones, like Nevada. Never afraid
to dream, your idea of America

remained what we'd seen in the
movies: fields where men keep
rounding the bases, cheeks red

with October chill. That first winter,
you said the snow looked warm.
And, now someone's promised you

a cot in a basement, you grin with
delight, as if the offer has redeemed
whatever wrong was done to you.

That One

How they picked back then was
by fondling the balls, the penis,
the calves, by running their
hands along the flanks as you
would horses, by looking into
the mouths and other orifices

pretending it wasn't exciting,
not the thrill of a Saturday
afternoon, not a good break
from the boring breeze blowing
through the weeping willows,
not a chance to see in the flesh

the cargo that came in chains
from the other side of the world,
passed through a door into hell,
the sea as if in a kettle boiling,
the green land disappearing
in a gulp, gone, the last hut

like a dream upon waking
to the touch of a strange hand,
the scent of a strange perfume
upon a skin so translucent, veins
like grey rivers snaking through
swamps of moss that hung in beards
off the magnolias, as in whispers

the wives advise, this one, this
one, for the bulbous knots on

his arms, for the pulsing drum
of the heart visible just beneath
the sternum, for the vacancy
in the rooms of his eyes as
they search for the wife, the child

not quite seven, for the ridge
of a spine that will answer the lash
with its own grimace, its own
inimitable dance in returning
to the tree where its navel string
climbs like a vine you can see now
if you go there, these many years after.

Taking My Brother Home

In the morning, I go to bury
his ashes in our mother's grave.
His request was to be thrown in the sea,
in a river, or in the Savannah.
But when we tried to do that with Uncle,
his remains blew back in our faces,
my cousin and I coated white,
like fish ready to fry.
I'll put my brother with our mom, write
his name on the headstone, under hers.
And hope he understands why here,
instead of blowing about,
stopping at friends' doors
(most of whom have passed away too),
yelling, *Open up, dammit,*
what you have to drink?

She Hasn't Seen Her Son in Years

For the third year, she's flying
to Chicago on Christmas day,
checking into that same hotel
with its view of the frozen river.

She'll sit in her room listening to
carols float down the hall as the
elevator doors open and close.
By midweek, she'll venture out for

a movie, leaving before the end.
She'll stay another two days, until
New Year's Eve, then check out,
party hat on top of her woolen

one. More than once, in the taxi
on the way to O'Hare, she'll imagine
she sees his face in the crowds. And
in the departure lounge, she'll try

his number again, between taking
pictures of Christmas decorations
and the stray dog running around
keeping the airport free of birds.

After the Flood

Only babies slept through the howling winds.
Morning finds the madman absent from his
post, though his bicycle bell keeps ringing.

The South is worse than the North; in some
quarters, no lights. It's also bad in Central,
where for now, the shooting has stopped.

Tomorrow the clinics will reopen. Cancer patients
will wait nervously for their chemo, observing
the lines to where the water came up. And

a badjohn* looking to settle a score will hear
that the man's child has died, and will end up
helping him kill the snake found under the bed.

* bad man

End Days

Now the wind approaches speeds of over
one hundred miles an hour, and water climbs up
to the arms of wheelchairs in the old folks' home.

One storm not quite done, another begins tearing
across the sea, an island waving its broken palms,
boats tethered to jetties that have drifted away.

And on a ship stranded inland, the manifest flutters
in the dead captain's hand, while his cargo of pigs
drowns in the wake of a Category 5 hurricane.

At such high frequencies, the rescuers cannot
hear the cries for help, cannot distinguish
between a cat mewling and the parrot in a cage

in a kitchen, its owner swimming towards where
the door was, remembered for its rusted hinges.

The Wind Dies Down

In the afternoon we go back as the wind
dies down, to find the goat still tethered
to a post at the end of a withered field,
our roof on top of a neighbor's.

How fierce, the herd that thundered
across the Atlantic, a sound like the
whipping of thick skin, followed by an
aggrieved howling. Then the water

poured from the separate rooms of
our houses, chamber pots clanging,
bedclothes decorating the main road
for everyone to see, and in the mud

a reddish-brown, drowned dog. A stern
quiet lies over all now, mattresses turned
to see if any child might be trapped, who
slept till the last minute, thumb in his mouth.

It's a pacifier for the ages, as we wonder
how the other islands fared, if people
are walking around, awakened into
the nothing promised us in the end.

Minding the Muse

after Robert Hass

You've mastered the long form,
followed it in and out of forests,
noted its markings on trees, and,
returning to cities, read at weddings,
helping yourself to wedding cake.

You've woken up to find yourself
surrounded by the sea, marooned
on a small island, asking directions,
surprised at knowing the language,
diphthong and all. The stars, as

you lost count and started over,
kept you company. You find as far
as the mountains are concerned,
there's no finite body, no actual
end. You've let your lines grow

like beards, not afraid to let them
touch the ground, trail their way
back, having seen where the
coffee you drink comes from,
forest fires hissing in evening rain.

Having studied the habits of ants,
you've learned the eternal
business of work, this gathering,
how we must join our sighs to
our singing, this feeding the queen.

What Now

for my brother

He comes up with two things
to test you, and before you can
answer, he's slapping his knee,
and shouting, *Gotcha!* Like, what's

the difference between behavior
and attitude. Who cares?
But long after he's done,
you find yourself pondering,

just to be ready when next
he comes. It's worse when he's
had a few. Then all your sense
goes flying, and you're caught

not knowing the difference
between region and area. Quick
now, while he dozes, leave the room,
put your books back in order,

for the answer's not there. Next,
he'll hum a tune, then ask you
about that flatted fifth, why it
breaks your heart, every time.

Men Only

The waiting room
at the prostate doctor's
is full of depressed-looking men
drinking extra cups of water

so they can pee
as the nurse stands behind them
with the contraption that measures
the girth of your penis

when you're done. The mind wills
the body to cooperate, the stream
to be strong. Later, before the intrusive
camera, your gland withdraws

as the technician tries
to distract you with stories
of her boyfriend who doesn't
want her doing this. *Breathe*, she says.

Outside, I recognize
more than one guy
from my neighborhood. We nod
disconsolately when the doc,

a sharp dresser, tells the nurse
to schedule someone else
for surgery. We toast each other
with more water.

The Artist as Immigrant

I keep hearing their prayers as they
lean against subway doors, and I
recall the tremble in my friend's voice

on the line from Ohio, hiding in his
dorm, after reading about some arrest
far from where he was studying, the girl

who said she would marry him changing
her mind at the last hour. And when
I let him stay at my place that summer,

he wanted no radio, no tv, fearing news
of anyone being rounded up. He painted
a mural on my wall and lived in it, while

on the basketball court outside were
guys from all over, yelling profanities in
strange accents. Now he's safely married,

living somewhere in Delaware. But his wife
admits there are nights he still wakes in terror,
scaring his grandson coming down the hall.

Elegy for Saheed Vassell

In his hand, the bathroom fixture
looked like a gun. In his mind, Utica Ave.
was a movie set, with shoppers
he could sneak up behind and, *Pow!*

he could scare them silly, run and tell his
cousin, how many he killed. But someone
dialed 911, and cops flooded the avenue,
as if the blue shipping barrels outside stores
had broken loose, while the man whom

everyone liked to see sweep and dance
with his broom, lay on the ground,
the piece of pipe in his hand, gazing
blindly at the sun, and then the stars,
and then, a late-rising moon.

Seven Beauties, Remembered

In South Trinidad one day,
a man walked past
the refinery guard,

climbed a ladder, and dove
into a tank of crude.
It took days to recover

his heartbroken body,
days of stirring until he
bobbed to the surface.

It took him longer
than the prisoner
in a Nazi compound

who ran between
the lines of inmates
and officers, diving

into a dumpster
full of human waste,
a move that left you

with your mouth open
long after the film
had gone on to

the next scene with
Mastroianni trying
in vain to fuck

the fat female
commandant, her boot
on his shoulder,

hardly able
to perform,
so weak he was.

The Side of the Road

Pastor Michael Briese of Maryland, at a funeral service for
long-time parishioner Agnes Hicks, told black mourners to
get out of his church. (theroot.com)

We know the dead can't feel,
but maybe they do, when an
angry relative stops the service
and has the undertaker

take the corpse to another
parlor. Or when the priest,
in the middle of the eulogy,
says, *Get out of my church*.

Before he died, my brother
said we could leave his body
at the roadside someplace,
if we didn't want

the expense or trouble.
Of course that's not what
we did. The pastor was
properly reverential. Black,

in his black robe. If anything,
he went on too long. I could
hear my brother saying
the side of the road is fine.

Rotting, for all to see, and
smell. This is how we looked
once, hanging from a tree.

Beloved

for Toni Morrison

The day you died, two deputies
led a black man into town
between their horses,

spectators lining both sides
of the street recalling the days
patterrollers brought runaways

back in chains, the clanking
heard long before the captives
appeared, like this man, limping,

the rope round his wrists tied to
the pommel of one of the saddles.
His eyes, fixed on a place far away,

made us feel he could have been
in one of those novels of yours,
the child a mother had let live.

The Blind Man Who Saw Through Us

for Steve Cannon

What I remember most of all
about the reading in your garden
is the treacherous fire escape
one had to descend to get there,

the lingering tremor in my legs
as I stood among the flowers,
the East Village pressing close.
From an upstairs window you

shouted, *Tell them about Walcott!*
About his experience west of here,
the thugs who kicked and scattered
his poems in the snow, your tone

chiding, as if I had been there, and
done nothing to help gather them in.
You were, and are, always on patrol:
rickety stairs, blindness—no excuses.

Blue Corn

for Susana Case

It was the staple of tribes making
their way across the plains and into
the hills, where their destiny was
written in the snow, wolf tracks and
howls, before the ascent to heaven,

blue, each kernel telling a story,
of death from disease, of the hero
Geronimo, his name breaking free,
wild horse of a warrior whose war cry
made the season of undoing long,

blue skies turning red for years,
elders going to wait for the blind
dealer in the place where he shuffles
his cards, deals the hooded one.
The Negroes chose this color for

sad songs, the whistles of trains, low
groans and absent smiles, *gone,*
the most prevalent word, women
looking through windows, fields
of maize hiding hollow logs, bodies

in the swamp, love in their hearts,
coming to the surface as gas. Blue,
the gas ring under the pot of coffee,
waking the worker in the morning,
the poet trying to make some

sense of it all. After all, it was a big
country, fish enough, meat cured
in the smokehouse. What was the
language of their signals, she wants
to know, what turned the corn blue?

Soufrière

Seen from above, our islands appear like
random realms of royal palms, broken off

from larger lands. On a field of heaving water,
we float, believing in signs and dreams,

the numbers that divine for us how many
stones are needed to build back Monserrat.

Once a year, love tosses our bodies from the
Carnival, into the vault of the volcano, and we

shade our eyes and see the coast we were
taken from, quivering with phantom pain.

The Susquehanna

is in danger of breaking its banks, in
that valley where you went to school,
learned to play the tuba, took a lover

under one of the bridges leading out
of the dark campus. There was never
enough heat in the house where you

lodged, I forget the family's name.
They were kind, but untidy, a flood of
clothes and toys always underfoot, a

dog that farted freely, and drooled.
News of the river widening every
day of this week of the blood moon

sends a tidewash of old images, of
the pudgy sophomore you claimed
was just a friend, who would surely

drown now, if the two of you tried
to run, scramble up the wet grass,
the muddy water rising inch by inch.

The Piano Teacher's Birthday

By August, she'd blocked hotel rooms, and by
November, she had sent out invites, pinwheels
stashed in a box below her bed. Tonight, standing

on the balcony of the hall that cost a fortune
to rent, watching the sparks fall after the starbursts,
her dress cut low in the back, she ignores the chill,

and responds tearfully to those men in tuxes and
women in gowns caught up in the romance of the
palms, two at each entrance guarded by waiters

with their shields of silver trays, her voice a
quaver: I've done this to mark the number
60, because lately this body has noted a stiffness

of the fingers over the keys, a tightness in the pedals.
And amid the laughter and applause there comes
from nearby the sound of the sea, as far out,

unseen, a man adrift in the current sends up
a flare, indistinguishable from her fireworks.

Trouble in Arima
after Kitch

Your art class meets
just off the Dial, not a long
walk, you say, and the streets
are well lit, and busy. But

that second night, as police
swarmed the taxi stand,
word was a maxi had been
driven into the hills, and

passengers made to hand
over everything: phones,
wallets, jewelry. The cops
boarded every vehicle

afterward, torchlights
flashed in every face,
even into the bag holding
your sketch pad, the

first set of drawings you
did. Your assignment
for tomorrow is to draw
the person opposite, whose

worry lines you shouldn't
erase, and whose heart
you should try to capture,
embroidered on his sleeve.

Resistance

The workmen in my kitchen are
tearing things apart. New cabinets,
though I loved the old, country-style
ones, the scalloped trim I painted two

shades of blue. I hide out in the bedroom,
the walls shaking as they pound and
break wood that comes away with creaks
and groans, nails human in their holding.

Outside, it's a hot one, protesters
on the move. I feel compelled to mention
them, their bravery. Only yesterday
I came across a picture in the paper,

of myself and students I'd encouraged
to march down a street in the Village.
It might have been for Mumia; the headline's
gone, and I don't remember the cause

exactly, or what we were yelling.
But now I'm thinking how
nothing gives way without breakage,
without some form of damage to the old,

the claw hammer in the hands of
the workman, the nail powerless as
he approaches. The battle for dignity rages
in the nights and days, the homeless joining

the campaign, the retired like me hunkered
down, taking notes, witnessing how there must
be dissent, and noise, the very floor coming up,
the policeman's foot in mid-kick, coming down.

My Father's Jacket

hangs on a line outside, on a day
when it is snowing. The shoulders
are soon covered with white, his
body absent between the lapels.

It is how I dream him, in this
place where he has never been.
I speak to his shadow, his scent
strongest at the times I am idle.

In his quiet way, he takes note
of my sadness, asks why I don't go
home, to the house that rises steeply
at the back, so the steps must climb

to meet the floor. It's where I fell
once, into a bucket, my whole body
fitting, like a small animal. He said,
Boy, and left me to my mother.

The jacket swings when the wind
blows, loose, dancing by itself, and
makes me remember the morning
of his funeral, when his friends sat

in the living room, and Telemac, his
closest, asked if he could have it,
with its frayed cuffs and collar,
the two top brass buttons missing.

Dónde está

for Derek Walcott, in memoriam

Only last week, I sent you new work,
thinking how many lines I should have
changed before you received them,
frowning, and asking the old question—
Dónde está la música, señor?

I had hoped you would read past the first
ten pages or so, getting to the good stuff,
glasses reflecting the evening light
coming off the Vigie headland, making sure
my endings were no longer shrill, that

they stopped, like the wooden
wheels of a donkey cart, the animal
knowing where, better than the driver.
I've been practicing, Derek, holding each word
like a dancer before the dip, in the backyards

where we boys got ready for the girls.
I did not paint at an early age, as you did.
I looked at the living portraits of uncles and aunts,
what the sagaboys* made of their rough-stitched,
determined selves. These are what

I sent you, Sir, in disguise, hoping they would
get through, that the winds might carry them
to where you sat facing the sea. I had no idea
they'd already arrived, and you had thrown up
your hands, impatient with one small error.

* *sharp dressers, ladies' men.*

Lightning Source UK Ltd.
Milton Keynes UK
UKHW010410230720
367020UK00001B/14